The Shocking Truth About Mom

Never before have any authors delved so deeply into the mysteries of Momhood. This amazing new book answers riddles that have plagued scientists for centuries:

• Why do Moms in different hemispheres who have never even exchanged recipes by mail serve macaroni and cheese on Thursdays?

• Why do all Moms instinctively know that washing silverware in cold water is the only way to remove egg yolk?

• Why does every language known to man contain a glyph, sound, or phrase that means "Someday when you have children of your own, you'll know what I'm talking about"?

The Mom Book is a giant step forward in the ongoing quest to achieve better communication between parent and child. It cannot help but make children finally realize that when Mom says, "Because I said so," she means it—and no ifs, ands, or buts!

The
Mom Book

Judith Victoria Jacklin
Deanne Rebecca Stillman
Anne Patricia Beatts

A DELL TRADE PAPERBACK

A DELL TRADE PAPERBACK
Published by
Dell Publishing
a division of
The Bantam Doubleday Dell Publishing Group, Inc.
666 Fifth Avenue
New York, New York 10103
*The section entitled "How to Talk like a Mother"
originally appeared in* Redbook.

Text copyright © 1983, 1986 by Judith Jacklin,
Deanne Stillman, Anne Beatts

Additional artwork by Judith Jacklin

Printed in the United States of America

Library of Congress Cataloging in Publication Data

Jacklin, Judith
  The mom book.

  1. Mothers—Anecdotes, facetiae, satire, etc.
I. Stillman, Deanne. II. Beatts, Anne III. Title.
PN6231.M68J3   1986   818'.5402
ISBN 0-440-53821-1
Library of Congress Catalog Card Number: 85-24716

One previous edition

May 1987

10 9 8 7 6 5 4 3

MV

To our moms,
without whom this book would not
have been possible.

Authors' Note

Although we've tried to describe the universal Mom, the astute reader will no doubt notice that most of our examples deal with mother-daughter relationships. We've done this for two reasons. One, we're daughters. And two, we feel that the mother-son relationship is one on which such noted male authorities on motherhood as Sophocles, Dr. Sigmund Freud, Philip Roth, and Prince have already commented so extensively that it would be impossible to top them.

Furthermore, we'd like to add a word about mothers-in-law and stepmothers. Most people seem to forget that in order to be a mother-in-law you must first be a mother—which means that anything Mom can do, a mother-in-law can do. And sometimes it can actually be easier to deal with your mother-in-law than your mom, especially when your mother-in-law takes your side in a family debate in order to make her son feel guilty.

As for stepmothers, we feel that they've gotten a bum rap from fairy tales (which have also unfairly elevated the godmother subclass). Evidently the Brothers Grimm weren't called that for nothing. What have those brothers got against stepmothers anyway? Why don't they just give them a break? Do they think it's easy to be a stepmother with some fancy godmother around all the time, promising impressionable youngsters that they'll live happily ever after? What do they think life is, a fairy tale?

Introduction

Everybody, all over the world, has one thing in common: a Mom. You only get one, so it's important that you take good care of her. There are hundreds of books on how to look after baby, but, until now, not one on how to look after Mom. That's why we created *The Mom Book*.

We have observed Mom in her native habitat for months at a time, and devoted countless hours to analyzing the resulting Mom-related data. Altogether, we have researched the subject of Mom for 110 years (the combined total of our ages, and we're not letting on who is how old—only our Moms know for sure, and they're not telling).

In the following pages we explore the state of Momhood. What is a Mom? Where does she come from? Will she ever go back there? And what time is the next train?

We offer insights into Mom's behavioral patterns: her language, her characteristics, and her habits (like making you show clean hands before dinner). We also tell you how to take care of Mom, how to get Mom to take care of you, and how to get her to stop taking care of you—although we're not really sure about this last one, because we haven't been too successful with it ourselves.

The Mom Book is not only for those who want to understand their Moms, but also for those Moms-to-be who want to get it right. After all, being a Mom takes time, patience, and a really good meatloaf recipe (see page 25).

We hope this book will help others as much in the reading as it helped us in the writing. For one thing, it provided us with an endless source of topics to call and talk to Mom about. And it should prove conclusively to all our Moms that we were paying attention, after all.

And Then
There Was Mom

N O one knows exactly when the first Mom appeared on the face of the earth. Some, namely Carl Sagan, say it was billions and billions of years ago, a theory that is partially supported by the existence of fossilized remains of Whitman's Samplers.

According to another popular theory, the first Mom was Eve, whom God created because Adam couldn't figure out how to make Cain and Abel clean up after themselves. Other students of history point to the first recorded indication of Mom, which appeared in the form of a recipe for chicken soup in the famous cave paintings at Lascaux.

Scholars agree that this primitive painting depicts Neanderthal Mom, enraged because she has told Neanderthal Dad five times that dinner is on the floor. Typically, he ignores her and keeps on chasing bison, an activity that was the pre-Ice Age equivalent of golf.

Regardless of when Mom made her first appearance, she has certainly left her mark. It's no coincidence that sailors down through the ages have immortalized Mom with colorful tattoos, which caused Mom to sigh with mingled pride and despair when she caught sight of them.

Famous Moms include Mother Hubbard, Mother Machree, Ma Barker, the Queen Mother, Moms Mabley, Mommie Dearest, Rose Kennedy, and the Virgin Mary. Moms may achieve fame as one half of a couple, such as Ma Kettle, or all on their own, like Mildred Pierce. There are mothers who are famous for what their sons did, like Gladys Presley, and those who are famous in their own right, like Mother Goose.

There are prolific mothers, like Mrs. Dionne, mother of the quints, Mrs. Warner, mother of the Brothers, and the old lady who lived in a shoe, mother of so many children she didn't know what to do. There are mothers who aren't even mothers, like Mother Teresa, and some mothers who aren't even women, like the Mothers of Invention. There's Mother Earth, Mother Russia, and Mother of Pearl, and take it from us, that Pearl is a wonderful homemaker who will make some young periodontist a fine wife someday.

One thing's for sure, Mom will never be an endangered species. We could go on listing memorable Moms until the cows come home. But we've got a book to finish, and we better get cracking, because never put off till tomorrow what you can do today.

Naming Mom

I N the beginning, Mom makes it easy for you by naming herself. She repeats her choice over and over until you catch on, and her name is likely to be the first word you say. Statistics show that it is also the word you repeat most often throughout your life, especially if you are Catholic, or Jewish.

Once you gain command of the language, you will probably want to start experimenting with other monickers. These will vary depending on how you feel about Mom at the time, or how you think Mom feels about you. Every Mom worth her salt will recognize immediately when the word "Mother!" is a term of endearment, and when it is an expletive, so watch your mouth, young lady, or I'm going to come up there and wash it out with soap.

The following are some of the most common names for Mom, with their meanings, uses, and derivations.

Mama. (mah'ma), *n*. That warm, soft person who picks you up when you cry. Prob. the first word you say, or at least the first word that baby dolls say.

Mommy. (mahm'mēe), *n. sing.*; *pl*. Mommies (mahm'mēeze). Part of her is higher than you can see, but she bends down to your level a lot. Orig. U.S. Usage most often accompanied by skirt-tugging.

Mom. (mahm), *n*. She still rules your life and doesn't realize that you're old enough to stay home without a baby-sitter. Deriv. of Mommy.

Mummy. (mum'mēe), *n. sing.*; *pl*. Mummies (mum'mēeze). A British and uppercrust var. of Mommy. Orig. Egyptian, i.e., what King Tut called his mother.

Mum. (mumm), *n*. What the Beatles called their mothers. Usually prefaced by "me."

Mumsie. (mumm'zēe), *n*. What Chatsworth Osborne, Jr., the spoiled rich kid on "Dobie Gillis," called his mother.

Maw. (mô), *n*. What Li'l Abner called his mother.

Mammy. (mam'ēee), *n*. What Al Jolson called his mother.

Maman. (mahmanh'), *n., Fr*. What Maurice Chevalier called his mother, and, incidentally, his last words. Perhaps this is why some people called Chevalier the French Jolson.

Naming Mom

I N the beginning, Mom makes it easy for you by naming herself. She, repeats her choice over and over until you catch on, and her name is likely to be the first word you say. Statistics show that it is also the word you repeat most often throughout your life, especially if you are Catholic, or Jewish.

Once you gain command of the language, you will probably want to start experimenting with other monickers. These will vary depending on how you feel about Mom at the time, or how you think Mom feels about you. Every Mom worth her salt will recognize immediately when the word "Mother!" is a term of endearment, and when it is an expletive, so watch your mouth, young lady, or I'm going to come up there and wash it out with soap.

The following are some of the most common names for Mom, with their meanings, uses, and derivations.

Mama. (mah′ma), *n*. That warm, soft person who picks you up when you cry. Prob. the first word you say, or at least the first word that baby dolls say.

Mommy. (mahm′mēe), *n. sing.*; *pl*. Mommies (mahm′mēeze). Part of her is higher than you can see, but she bends down to your level a lot. Orig. U.S. Usage most often accompanied by skirt-tugging.

Mom. (mahm), *n*. She still rules your life and doesn't realize that you're old enough to stay home without a baby-sitter. Deriv. of Mommy.

Mummy. (mum′mēe), *n. sing.*; *pl*. Mummies (mum′mēeze). A British and uppercrust var. of Mommy. Orig. Egyptian, i.e., what King Tut called his mother.

Mum. (mumm), *n*. What the Beatles called their mothers. Usually prefaced by "me."

Mumsie. (mumm′zēe), *n*. What Chatsworth Osborne, Jr., the spoiled rich kid on "Dobie Gillis," called his mother.

Maw. (mô), *n*. What Li'l Abner called his mother.

Mammy. (mam′ēee), *n*. What Al Jolson called his mother.

Maman. (mahmanh′), *n., Fr*. What Maurice Chevalier called his mother, and, incidentally, his last words. Perhaps this is why some people called Chevalier the French Jolson.

Mither. (mĭth′ar), *n.*, *Scot. and N. Eng.* What Lord Randal called his mother in the old Scottish folk song "Lord Randal My Son." Unfortunately, neither Jolson nor Chevalier ever recorded this tune, or it might have been a chart-topper.

Mutha. (muth′uh), *n.*, *Bl.* A name that doesn't usually refer to your mother. Most often a term of hostility, as in "You mutha!"

Mother. (mŭth′er), *n.* 1. The woman from whom you're hoping to borrow the car tonight. 2. Also used to refer to the Holy Virgin, Mother Mary, the one you hope will come to you, speaking words of wisdom, let it be, let it be.

Ma. (mah), *n.*; or (mah·ah·ah·ah, depending on urgency of request). Var. of Mother; ex.: Mrs. Kettle. Useful abbr. for when Mom is at the other end of the house, or vacuuming.

Mom's First Name. (mahmz ferst nāme), *n.* Used by liberated children and impudent brats; until you reach the age your Mom was when she had you, at which point it becomes acceptable to some people.

Mrs. Your Last Name Here. (mis′iz yōor lăst năm hîr), *n.* There comes a point in your life when you realize that your mother isn't Mommy to everyone. She's not always known as your mother; sometimes she's Dad's wife. You seldom call her by this name, but it comes in handy when signing official documents in her behalf, such as report cards and notes to teacher.

She. (shēe), *pron.* Otherwise known as the cat's mother.

The Seven Ages of Mom

HOW many times has your Mom told you, "You're just going through a phase"? Well, like you, Mom has her phases too, governed not by the moon but by how old you happen to be at the time. Whenever Mom does something that upsets you, just remember: She'll grow out of it.

When you are . . .

I. Newborn through two years old.	Mom can do no wrong. She is the sun around which your tiny universe revolves, the ever-present source of all food, heat, light, and warmth. Mommy loves her itty-bitty sweetheart sooo much. Isn't it the most beautiful baby you've ever seen?
II. A toddler through kindergarten.	Mom starts to use the word "no," and sometimes slaps, especially when you reach up to touch the pretty china bird figurines. Mom becomes strangely obsessive about your bathroom habits, and insists on introducing you to Mr. Toidy.
III. In grade school.	Surprise! Mom thinks it's time for you to go to school and get plasticine rubbed in your hair. After a while, you get used to it, but there's still no one like Mom. On the other hand, if she got sick and Miss McNulty took over for a few days, it wouldn't be so bad. She's younger than Mom, and might understand why you absolutely must have a Strawberry Shortcake pencil case before to-morrow or you'll be so embarrassed you can never show your face in school again.

IV. A teen-ager.	Mom is impossible. There is virtually nothing that she can do that doesn't embarrass you. She's gauche, old hat, and gets really upset when you borrow her makeup. Besides, she has absolutely no taste in music, and just doesn't understand why it's imperative that she stay off the phone from the time you get home from school until the time you leave for school the next morning. This is a very difficult period for both of you, and one that is best handled by staying in your room with the door shut, sleeping or watching MTV.
V. College age through twenty-five.	Mom starts to improve. You realize what a wonderful cook and laundress she is, but her telephone manners still leave something to be desired: every phone conversation with Mom begins, "I didn't wake you, did I?" About this time, Mom takes an abnormal interest in your living arrangements and wants to know the gender, sexual preference, and credit rating of anyone who so much as takes a nap on your foldout couch. "Are you supporting all of your friends? Don't they have mothers of their own?"
VI. Twenty-five through thirty-five.	Mom gets younger and her taste in music takes a turn for the better. She wants to be your friend, but the main thing you have in common is an interest in you. On the other hand, so what if she thinks your loft bed should have a guardrail, who else can you call after 11:00 P.M. when you want to know how to clarify butter?
VII. Thirty-five and beyond.	Mom may turn out all right, after all. Many of the things she told you make a lot of sense in the long run. In fact, you often find yourself sympathizing with her point of view, especially about credit ratings and loft beds. Mom's really very sweet, and looks young for her age, especially after you've given her a perm. You just wish she'd exercise more, and you worry when you don't hear from her for two or three days. She could be lying in a ditch somewhere.

Mom's First Years

EVERYONE remembers their first-grade teacher, their first kiss, and their first hangover. Mom has a lot of firsts to celebrate, too, but she's paying so much attention to you, she doesn't think to record her important firsts. So we've done it for her. Now the two of you can cherish those wonderful moments in years to come. Plus this gives you something to bring out and embarrass her with in front of company when she brings out your baby book.

Mom's First Word:
   "No."
   Although this is the first word to be strongly imprinted on Baby's consciousness, Mom undoubtedly said a lot of nicer things to you before you were old enough to understand them. Coincidentally, "no" is also Mom's last word on the subject, and she doesn't want to hear another peep out of you, young lady.

Mom's Sleeping Pattern
   Whenever Baby's asleep, Mom is too, except for the times she has to stay up with Dad. In Baby's first year, Mom yawns a lot whenever she has to stay up later than a quarter past Baby.

Mom's Feeding Habits
   Mom finds herself eating a lot of baby food such as strained vegetables and soggy arrowroot cookies, both in an attempt to encourage Baby to eat ("One spoonful for me, and one for you! Mmmm . . . delicious!") and also because Mom can't stand to see anything go to waste, not even crusts. Even when Mom goes out, she doesn't get to eat like a regular person, because while she's at the phone making sure Baby's okay, the waiter clears away her unfinished shrimp cocktail.

Mom Waves Bye-Bye:
   The first time she has to go-go.

Mom's First Photo:

Mom's First Step:
The cha-cha.

Mom's First Bath
By the end of Baby's first year, Mom finally has enough time to herself to take a bath instead of a shower.

Mom's First Tantrum
It occurs when Mom's first bath is interrupted by Baby deciding that this would be the ideal moment to take everything out from under the kitchen sink and play with it, instead of having a nap.

Mom's Favorite Toys and Games
Mom enjoys pointing to herself and saying "Mommy" to Baby. Mom also likes Pat-a-cake, Peekaboo, and Tickle. When Baby is a little older, Mom encourages quiet games, and becomes particularly fond of Hide-and-seek. Oddly enough, it takes longer and longer for Mom to find Baby the more often she plays this game.

Mom's First Day at School
Mom comes to your classroom and spends a whole hour with her knees squeezed under one of those little desks. She insists that your painting is the only one where you can tell it's a tree.

New Mom

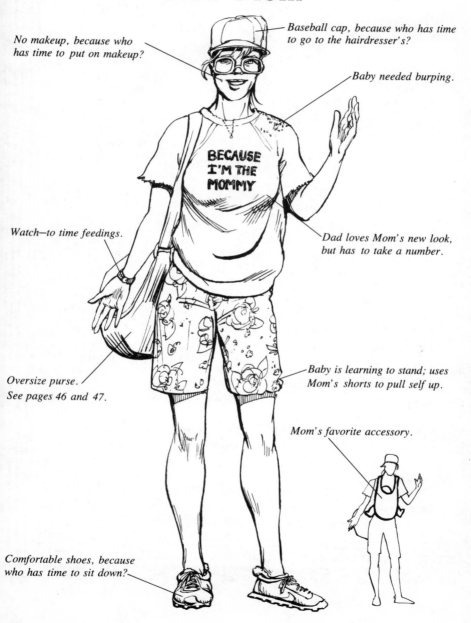

No makeup, because who has time to put on makeup?

Baseball cap, because who has time to go to the hairdresser's?

Baby needed burping.

BECAUSE I'M THE MOMMY

Watch—to time feedings.

Dad loves Mom's new look, but has to take a number.

Oversize purse. See pages 46 and 47.

Baby is learning to stand; uses Mom's shorts to pull self up.

Mom's favorite accessory.

Comfortable shoes, because who has time to sit down?

Mom's Hopes and Fears

SOMETIMES it may seem as though Mom has more fears than hopes, but that's just because her main hope is that her fears won't come true. Growing up with Mom, you learn a lot about what spooks her from the warning signals she broadcasts continuously over WMOM, the radio station to which you became a lifetime subscriber at birth. At times Mom's warning is just a test; other times it's a real emergency. But you probably won't be able to tell the difference until you're grown up, so pay attention and do what Mom says, not what she does.

Mom's Afraid That . . .
>   You're overweight.
>   You're underweight.
>   You're growing too fast.
>   You're not growing fast enough.
>   You're studying too hard.
>   You're not studying hard enough.
>   You're working too hard.
>   You're not working hard enough.
>   You'll tip your chair over backward and split your head open and
>   have to be rushed to the hospital.
>   You'll stick a fork in the toaster and be electrocuted.
>   You'll gulp your food and choke to death.
>   You'll break your teeth chewing ice.
>   You'll eat her out of house and home.
>   You don't eat enough to keep a bird alive.
>   You'll get a disease from not washing your hands before dinner.
>   You'll get a disease from kissing your pet.
>   You'll pick your scabs and be permanently disfigured.

You'll squeeze a pimple and die of a brain hemorrhage.

Your ears will get so dirty, you'll be able to grow potatoes in them.

You'll put beans in your nose and not be able to get them out and have to be rushed to the hospital.

You'll swallow your gum and choke to death.

You'll go swimming too soon after eating and get stomach cramps and drown.

You'll go out without a sweater and catch your death of cold.

You'll go out with wet hair and die of pneumonia.

You'll go barefoot and step on a rusty nail and get lockjaw and won't be able to eat and starve to death.

You'll run while sucking a lollipop and fall down and puncture the roof of your mouth and have to be rushed to the hospital.

You'll forget to look both ways while crossing the street and never know what hit you until it's too late.

You'll accept candy from a stranger and Mom will never see you again.

You'll take the emergency brake off while playing in the car and roll into traffic.

You'll lose your arm hanging out the car window.

You'll get carsick if you read, and throw up all over the backseat.

You'll ruin your eyes reading in that light.

You'll go deaf listening to music that loud.

You'll rot your brain if you read too many comics.

You'll drop the phone in the bathtub and electrocute yourself.

Your ear will become permanently attached to the phone.

Your face will get stuck in that position.

You'll get a swelled head.

You'll get too big for your breeches.

Your tight jeans will squeeze your reproductive organs and you'll never be able to have children.

Your tight jeans will result in your having children too young.

You'll put her and Dad in the poorhouse.

You'll be the death of her.

You'll be late for your own funeral.

How to Talk
like a Mother

MOTHERS are very special people. So special, in fact, that they have their very own language. We call it "the mother tongue." Such phrases as "It's way past your bedtime" and "Right where you left it" seem to spring spontaneously from the mouth of anyone who has ever experienced maternity.

Scientists speculate that this universal language is locked in the human genetic code and passed on from mother to daughter, activated at the moment of giving birth by an as yet unnamed female hormone—we vote to call it Cheryl.

This theory, however, does not explain to our satisfaction why mothers of adopted children, and even women who find themselves left in charge of a child for merely an hour or two, also become mysteriously fluent in the same idiom. Perhaps Cheryl is dormant until activated by contact with someone capable of repeating the word "why?" two hundred times in as many minutes.

But who knows? Maybe if we could just *buckle down, turn off that radio, and get cracking,* we might be able to get some work done and find a solution to this perplexing problem. Or maybe we should just *ask your father about it when he gets home.*

In the meantime, we have compiled a short lexicon of some of the most recognizable and hilarious phrases our own mothers have used. Phrases that—when we are around anyone who is under the age of twelve—we sometimes find ourselves using as well.

Take this list to your room and study it *thoroughly,* because if you don't think it's hysterically funny, *you have only yourself to blame, young lady.*

Authors' Note: The words "young lady" may be added for empha-sis to any of the following phrases, as in "Stop that, young lady!" When Mom is really mad, "young lady" may be replaced by a proper name: "Rhonda Oglesby! Stop that immediately!" In ex-treme cases, the full name, middle name included, may be substi-tuted: "Rhonda May Oglesby! Stop that at once! And I mean it!" And with the right emphasis, the name alone may be sufficient, viz.: "Rhonda May Oglesby!" This last is usually delivered in a tone of controlled hysteria.

Rhetorical Mom

Mom's curiosity never flags. There's nothing she likes better than asking you questions. However, the worst mistake you can make with Rhetorical Mom is to try to answer any of them. *Who do you think you are anyway, Miss Smarty-pants?*

Can't you get that hair out of your eyes?
You have such a pretty face, why hide it?
Do you want to have a scar?
Is that any way for a young lady to
  sit/act/talk/look/speak/dress/behave?
Is *that* what you're wearing?
What if you were in an accident and had to go to the hospital and
  you were wearing dirty underwear?
Where's the fire?
Where do you think you're going at this hour?
Do you know what time it is?
Are you still up?
Are you asleep?
Whose brilliant idea was this?
Who's going to clean up this mess?
Who do you think you're fooling?
Do you think I'm just the maid around here?

Dr. Mom

Every Mom spends a major portion of her Momhood dispensing time-honored medical information and health tips. Though most Moms are licensed to write prescriptions only for TLC and plenty of liquids, they are always willing to make house calls. Although Dr. Mom is a bit of a worrywart, there is one occasion on which her diagnosis is invariably optimistic: First thing Monday morning when you're getting ready *not* to go to school, Mom is likely to say: *"You don't have a temperature."* Here is more of Dr. Mom's medical vocabulary:

Where does it hurt?
Is it an ache, or a pain?
Let me feel your forehead.
How do you know you don't like it if you haven't tried it?
Did you finish everything on your plate?
Why don't you go outside and get some fresh air?
A growing girl needs her beauty sleep.

Philosopher Mom

Mom has spent a lot of time thinking about a lot of things, especially when you were an adorable baby who couldn't talk back. As a result, Philosopher Mom has a pantryful of stock phrases with which she seasons your life. Here are a few:

Rome wasn't built in a day.
Money doesn't grow on trees.
Don't put all your eggs in one basket.
Don't cry over spilt milk.
You can't have your cake and eat it too.
Idle hands are the devil's playground.
Every cloud has a silver lining.
There are plenty of fish in the sea.
You don't just marry a man; you marry his whole family.
Patience is a virtue.
Ignorance is bliss.
Since God couldn't be everywhere at once, he created mothers.

Comedian Mom

Where would Mom be without her sense of humor? Her clever quips stand her in good stead on numerous occasions. In fact, Comedian Mom is likely to take the stage when you least expect it—for instance, in the middle of an argument. Don't be embarrassed when Mom tries out some of her best material on your friends—their Moms do it too.

Try a little elbow grease.
You make a better door than a window.
You'd forget your head if it weren't screwed on.
Don't you want to become a member of the clean-plate club?
How would you like it if your face got stuck in that position?
A little bird told me.
If you think that's so funny, you can just go laugh in your room.

Mrs. Mom

A Mom is often a wife as well as a mother. This secondary role occasionally takes her away from her maternal duties, but it can also provide her with another, usually invisible, authority to invoke besides the Deity.

I'm afraid I'm going to have to phone your father.
  (Wrong. She's not afraid; you're the one who's afraid.)
Wait till your father gets home.
Do *you* want to tell your father what you did today?
It would break your father's heart.
Your father would have a heart attack.
It would kill your father.
Well, all right. Just don't tell your father.

Sympathetic Mom

Mom is often concerned with your plight, and does her best to help out. Sometimes, however, Sympathetic Mom's sympathy seems misplaced, and instead of making you feel better, it confirms your worst fears. But don't worry, *you'll understand when you're older*. After all, Mom was a daughter once herself.

It'll clear up when you're older.
You'll grow into it.
You'll grow out of it.
That's just baby fat.
You're just going through an awkward stage.
Don't worry, dear, you have good bone structure.
You were always my favorite, but don't tell your sister.
You can never do anything to make me not love you.
You've got your whole life ahead of you.

Pathetic Mom

Even Mom has her down days, and when she's down, she's usually down on you as well as on herself. Pathetic Mom can pluck at your heartstrings with the skill of Itzhak Perlman playing first violin in Tchaikovsky's *Symphonie Pathétique. And you deserve it, you thankless child, you!*

No one loves me.
Why listen to me? I'm just your mother.
I had visions of you splattered all over the highway.
I suppose you won't be happy until someone gets hurt.
I suppose you're happy now.
I just don't understand you anymore.
You'll be sorry when I decide to pick up and leave.
All I'm asking for is a little common courtesy.
Wait till you have a daughter of your own.
Someday you'll thank me.

Dear Mom

You don't have to read Ann Landers if you've a Mom in the house. Dear Mom is a walking encyclopedia of helpful hints for every social situation, from grooming to dating. And best of all, her advice is tailor-made for you, because *no one knows you better than your mother*.

Don't forget to send a thank-you note.
As long as you have good shoes and a good purse, it doesn't matter what else you're wearing.

A lady never raises her voice.
It's impolite to whisper.
Black goes with anything.
This is just puppy love.
You'll know when the real thing comes along.

Military Mom

There are moments when Mom has no time for discussion, because *somebody's gotta take on a little responsibility around here*. And if you don't snap to it, Military Mom will want to know the reason why. Mom may go through several incarnations as she rises through the ranks, hanging tougher and tougher throughout the week. On Saturday, when you're trying to get a little extra shut-eye, Mom is likely to wake you with a bugle and turn your tranquil home into a boot camp. *So get a move on*, or you'll find yourself doing double KP.

Sergeant Mom

Act your age.
Don't slouch.
Take a sweater.
Button your coat.
Don't be a smart aleck.
Wipe that grin off your face, buster.
Straighten up and fly right.
Shape up or ship out.
On the double.
Pronto.
March.
Mush.
Not so fast.
Simmer down.
Relax!
No roughhousing.
Don't play with your food.
Don't talk with your mouth full.
Don't touch yourself there.
Grow up, for Pete's sake.

General Mom

Get out of my hair.
See where that'll get you.
I'm coming in there.
No allowance for a week/month/year.
No daughter of mine is going to stay out all night at
    parties with boys/wear jeans that tight/dye her hair green for
    St. Patrick's Day.
This is my house, and as long as you live here, you'll
    abide by my rules.
What do you mean you "found" it?
You've got another think coming.
If I've told you once, I've told you a thousand times.
Don't start with me.
I've had it up to here.
No! I'm not kidding this time.
No! And I mean it.
We'll see.

Four-star-general Mom

I said no, capital N-O.
No ifs, ands, or buts.
Over my dead body.
I'm not going to tell you a second time.
I don't want to hear another word on the subject.
That's that.
End of discussion.
Period.

How to Drive
like a Mother

A Mom is someone who, when coming to an abrupt stop, automatically puts her arm out to protect tiny passengers, even when there aren't any.

FAR be it from us to promulgate the myth of women drivers; in fact, we may all owe our lives to Mom's skill behind the wheel. But it cannot be denied that Mom has a lot on her hands besides driving gloves when it's her turn in the carpool. It's not easy to stop a fight, wipe somebody's nose, hand out Bubble Yum, keep the dog from jumping out the window, and find lunch money while making an illegal U-turn to go back and retrieve Vanessa's Little League cap that Adam threw out of the sunroof when no one was looking.

Long car trips offer new challenges to Mom's ingenuity. Now she has to entertain her children as well as get them somewhere. Guess who invented the license plate game?

Mom doesn't leave home without:

Comics

Coloring books

Crayons

Deck of cards

Walkman (It's ideal to have one for each child; however, if this is a strain on the family budget, the kids can double up with an extra set of headphones. This gives Mom an opportunity to tune in to her favorite easy-listening station. It could be her only quiet time, so it's important to remember the extra batteries.)

Stuffed animals, such as Koosa the Cabbage Patch animal, the CareBear cousins, and Pound Puppies. (For those still young enough to refer to all forms of life as "Kitty," there are indeterminable furry creatures known as Wuzzles. And for those who have only recently developed the squeeze reflex, there are Globug dolls, which light up when you squeeze them—a form of conditioning that can only lead to disappointment and confusion in future sexual encounters.)

Dolls, such as Chatty Patty, Strawberry Shortcake, Rainbow Brite, Golden Girl, and Starfairy. (Mom would be well advised to stock the first-aid kit with insulin to offset the sugar shock brought on by the presence of so many cute things in one motor vehicle.)

Action figures, such as Dinobots, Gobots, and the He-Man Masters of the Universe series, including: Skeletor, Two Bad, and Whiplash, which is what Mom may get when she turns around and tells Adam to stop hitting Vanessa over the head with Clawful.

Pets (Mom might question the entertainment value of pets, but wouldn't she prefer that the kids tormented Bowser instead of her?)

Of course, we haven't bothered to mention the basics that Mom never forgets: gum, Kleenex, Handi-Wipes, baby aspirin, motion sickness pills, Bactine, juice, snacks, pillows, blankets, towels, etc. In fact, family size may have diminished in inverse ratio to the NMTTSG* per family unit, as it is impossible to fit all these things into a tiny little Japanese car and still have room for the kids.

The logistics of travel with children are complicated by the amazing ability of children to control their bladders until moments after Dad has pulled out of the Will Rogers Rest Stop and is trying to make it to the Petrified Teacup before nightfall. Failing corrective surgery, Mom will frequently find herself running the water and saying, "I want you to go to the bathroom right now, whether you need to or not."

In early Momhood, Mom worries most about the safety of her children. Later she worries most about the safety of her vehicle in the hands of hyperactive teens with hormones on the rampage who are liable to wrap themselves around a telephone pole and end up lying in a ditch somewhere if they don't keep both eyes on the road and both hands on the wheel at all times, young lady.

Of course, there is an intermediary stage through which it is safest to speed quickly, but which can best be summed up by the phrase "Do I look like your chauffeur?"

Don't be fooled into thinking that hiring a chauffeur would be a solution to this problem, since then arguments would ensue not only about the availability of the car but also about the availability of the chauffeur.

---

*Number of Miles Traveled to See Grandma

When It's Your Turn
to Take Care of Mom

WHO among us has not been rescued from the land of sore throats, runny noses, and stomachaches by good old Mom? Yes, her chicken soup never fails to purge the most persistent grippe; her hand on your forehead always seems to chase that temperature away, even while she's taking it.

But then comes that awful day when Mom takes to her own bed in pain. What's wrong with Mom? How is it possible that the person who is always there to minister to your needs is herself in need of aid? Can it be that Mom is actually sick, or is she just faking it?

First of all, even if Mom is faking it, she fakes it less frequently than you do, so it's advisable to indulge what is, after all, a not unnatural desire to be mothered. But let's assume that Mom isn't faking it. Let's assume that Mom is in bed with "some sort of bug, probably just a twenty-four-hour thing, I'm sure I'll be over it in no time." In other words, Mom has the flu. Here are a few tips for the neophyte nurse, which, of course, we have all learned from the original nurse herself—Mom.

Take the TV from your room and set it up on Mom's dresser. Tune it to her favorite soap opera, and promise not to change it to MTV, even if she falls asleep.

Figure out how to boil water and make Mom some tea. Figure out how to slice a lemon, and put some in it. Don't forget the honey, if you can figure out how to pry the lid off the jar (and if you can't, don't worry about it, because Mom can't get it off either; that's why the stuff has been sitting in the cupboard for two years, anyway).

Make dinner for Dad and pack your brother's lunch box. These two activities will probably cause so much chaos that Mom will be down in the kitchen before you can say, "What's wrong with spaghetti and ketchup?," scuttling around in her terry robe and scuffies, getting better before your very eyes. If she sneezes a few times in the direction of the food, don't worry: you might catch her cold, but guess who will be there to take care of it?

Mom Cuisine

N O ifs, ands, or buts, nobody can cook like Mom, and we don't mean maybe! Mom specializes in hearty meals that put meat on your bones and color in your cheeks. And although she tends to go a little heavy on the carbos, white sugar, and salt, who can resist such mouth-watering signature dishes as Mom's own Kraft macaroni and cheese casserole with crumbled Pringle's on top?

Three-star Mom Cuisine

The thoroughly modern Mom may adapt the following recipes for a food processor or a microwave, but we can only pass them along to you the way our Moms handed them down to us. They're palate-pleasers, every one. So polish up your silverware, and get ready for some delicious, nutritious treats.

This highly visual dish makes an equally good appetizer, side salad, or even dessert. Children will enjoy helping to prepare it, especially if they can drink the cherry juice. This is one dish not found in any restaurant!

Candle Salad (Serves 4)
2 bananas, lettuce leaves, pineapple rings, 2 maraschino cherries (red)

Arrange the lettuce leaves to form four cups
Peel and cut both bananas in half horizontally.
Place one pineapple ring on each lettuce cup
Stand up each banana half in the center of each pineapple ring and put half a cherry on top.
Serve to applause

Meatloaf Surprise   Bake at 350°F for 1-1½ hours
(Serves 4 w/some left over)
1 lb hamburger, 1 egg, ½ cup breadcrumbs, ½ cup cornflake crumbs, ketchup, Worcestershire sauce, Salt + pepper to taste
Surprise: could be anything in the house, from broccoli to canned corn or even, for a taste of the Orient, water chestnuts.
Combine ingredients, except for cornflake crumbs, in a mixing bowl. Pat into meatloaf pan. Top w/cornflake crumbs + an eye-catching ketchup design

Meatloaf is hardly a tired old standby when the savvy Mom livens it up with an element of surprise. This dish is also an excellent way to use up leftovers. Dad, who may be less surprised than most to see yesterday's brussels sprouts turning up in the meatloaf, can eat around the surprise. Leftover meatloaf can make a successful comeback as lunch-box sandwiches and surprise everyone again.

Nouvelle Mom Cuisine

Mom's inventiveness in the kitchen rivals that of the finest French chefs when it comes to creating dishes that will appeal to the finicky palate of a four-year-old. In her hands, the humble hot dog is transformed into a variety of child-pleasing treats.

This tasty combo, which Mom says goes together like a horse and carriage, can be served *en casserole* as either a hearty lunch or a light supper. It's economical, nourishing, and easy-to-fix, and keeps everyone regular. The cowboy connotations of beans help to make them popular with Mom's little cowboy or cowgirl. Their other attributes, which it would be bad manners to discuss at the dinner table, were immortalized in the famous campfire scene from *Blazing Saddles*. Kids will find this phenomenon as much fun as the film's ever-youthful director, Mel Brooks, but Mom best bear in mind that beans are not a dish to serve on a rainy day.

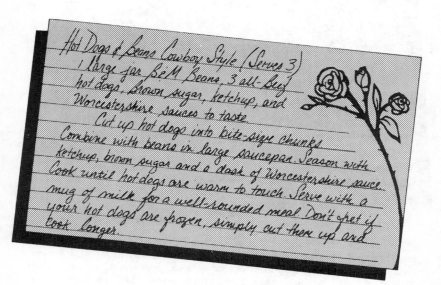

Hot Dogs & Beans Cowboy Style (Serves 3)
1 large jar B&M Beans, 3 all-Beef
hot dogs. Brown sugar, ketchup, and
Worcestershire sauces to taste.
Cut up hot dogs into bite-size chunks
Combine with beans in large saucepan Season with
ketchup, brown sugar and a dash of Worcestershire sauce.
Cook until hot dogs are warm to touch Serve with a
mug of milk for a well-rounded meal Don't fret if
your hot dogs are frozen, simply cut them up and
cook longer.

Mom's Kitchen Kut-ups

Although Mom often tells you not to play with your food, she also contradicts herself by creating food that seems to say, "C'mon and play with me!" How else would you explain cookie cutters? Then there are gingerbread men, pancake boys, and alphabet soup. Mom sometimes even goes so far as to suggest that the mashed potatoes are mountains and the gravy is a river, which would make you God. Only fair, since Mom gets to be Santa Claus, the Tooth Fairy, and the Easter Bunny. Around Eastertime, Mom demonstrates that she isn't plagued in the slightest by that hobgoblin of small minds, consistency, when she turns something you've already played with into food.

This dish provides a handy way of disposing of leftover Easter eggs. It goes well with any meal and also can be served as a snack. You might want to increase the quantities in this recipe, depending on the size of your family and the number of dyed eggs in your refrigerator on Easter Monday.

Rainbow Deviled Eggs

6 eggs, food coloring, mayonnaise, Worcestershire sauce, Tabasco, paprika, RealLemon lemon juice (optional)

Shell eggs. Place two eggs each in bowls containing red, blue, + orange food coloring. Let soak until eggs have changed color. Remove, slice in half lengthwise, + empty yolks into bowl. Add five tbsp. of mayonnaise, a dash of Worcestershire sauce, a few drops of Tabasco, paprika, and lemon juice. Stir with fork until smooth. Fill egg halves with mixture. Serve to "oohs" + "aahs."

Economical and easy-to-fix, this one-burner main dish is popular with every-one, including Grandma, who finds it easy on her dentures. And just laugh off the inevitable disgusting similes that teen-aged members of the family are likely to employ. Once they taste this dish, they'll love it!

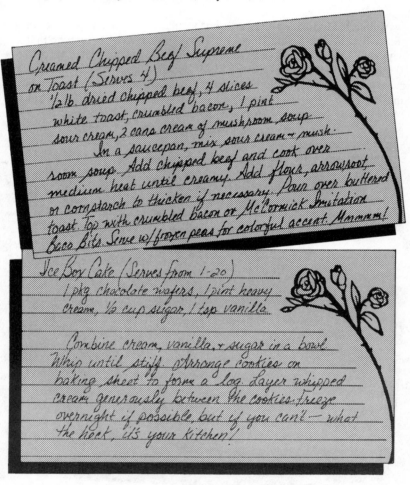

Creamed Chipped Beef Supreme
on Toast (Serves 4)
½ lb. dried chipped beef, 4 slices
white toast, crumbled bacon, 1 pint
sour cream, 2 cans cream of mushroom soup
    In a saucepan, mix sour cream + mush-
room soup. Add chipped beef and cook over
medium heat until creamy. Add flour, arrowroot,
or cornstarch to thicken if necessary. Pour over buttered
toast. Top with crumbled bacon or McCormick Imitation
Baco Bits. Serve w/ frozen peas for colorful accent. Mmmmm!

Ice Box Cake (Serves from 1-20)
1 pkg. chocolate wafers, 1 pint heavy
cream, ½ cup sugar, 1 tsp vanilla

    Combine cream, vanilla, + sugar in a bowl.
Whip until stiff. Arrange cookies on
baking sheet to form a "log." Layer whipped
cream generously between the cookies. Freeze
overnight if possible, but if you can't — what
the heck, it's your kitchen!

This versatile dessert is perfect for company dinners, the gardening club luncheon, a teen's slumber party, or whenever you feel like getting a fantastic sugar buzz.

This dish lacks the explosive quality of the preceding recipe, but is excellent for a rainy day, also known as Campbell's Soup Weather. No problem getting kids to eat their veggies with this dish. It's "m-m-m good!"

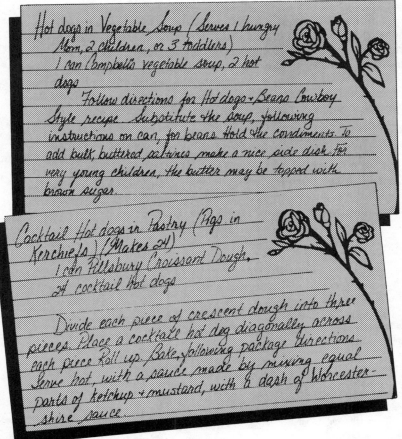

Hot dogs in Vegetable Soup (Serves 1 hungry Mom, 2 children, or 3 toddlers)
1 can Campbell's vegetable soup, 2 hot dogs

Follow directions for Hot dogs + Beans Cowboy Style recipe. Substitute the soup, following instructions on can, for beans. Hold the condiments. To add bulk, buttered saltines make a nice side dish. For very young children, the butter may be topped with brown sugar.

Cocktail Hot dogs in Pastry (Pigs in Kerchiefs) (Makes 24)
1 can Pillsbury Croissant Dough,
24 cocktail hot dogs

Divide each piece of crescent dough into three pieces. Place a cocktail hot dog diagonally across each piece. Roll up. Bake, following package directions. Serve hot, with a sauce made by mixing equal parts of ketchup + mustard, with a dash of Worcestershire sauce.

This is essentially a grown-up food to be served as a cocktail party snack or appetizer. However, both the preparation and the serving of this dish are easy for little hands, and provide a convenient way for Mom to involve the kids in a grown-up activity. While the grown-ups are chatting, the kids can pass around the hors d'oeuvres and garner compliments on their culinary skills. If one or two of these tempting tidbits find their way into little tummies, no need to worry, because after all, they're only hot dogs.

Lazy Mom Cuisine

It is understandable why Mom might sometimes feel like having someone else cook dinner, busy as she is with her children, her marriage, her career, her volunteer work, her exercise class, not to mention trying to find a spare five minutes to have sex with Dad every now and then. Three of Mom's favorite substitute chefs are Chef Boy•ar•dee, Colonel Sanders, and Ronald McDonald. However, any Lazy Mom worth her salt will vary this menu with TV dinners, frozen pot pies, pizza, and Chinese take-out.

It's easy to get children to eat this food. The problem is, once they've been trained to tinfoil, it's difficult to get them to eat off a plate with silverware again when company comes over. Although junk food can be a nutritious substitute for Mom's home cooking, Mom will never hang up her apron altogether, because when you grow up and move away, Mom wants you to miss her, not Arthur Treacher.

The Migratory Path of Leftovers
Through the Refrigerator

1 Shrink-wrapped frozen turkey on sale after Thanksgiving at 89 cents a pound at Safeway.

2 Leftover roast turkey on platter. Kids and Dad surreptitiously lift Saran Wrap, causing Mom to say, "If you keep picking at that, there'll be nothing but dark meat left for your lunchbox sandwiches."

3 Turkey soup, with no white meat in it.

4 Turkey broth in Tupperware, saved in order to use Tupperware.

5 Rendered turkey fat in glass mayonnaise jar, saved in case anyone comes up with a use for turkey fat.

6 Turkey bones, saved to be used as a base for more turkey broth, in case Mom runs out.

7 Turkey casserole, supplemented by tuna and served on a night when Dad's on a business trip and Junior's at the ballgame. Mom eats a third of it alone, in front of the TV.

8 Despite Junior's pleas that Mom save the moldy casserole for the science fair, Mom tosses it.

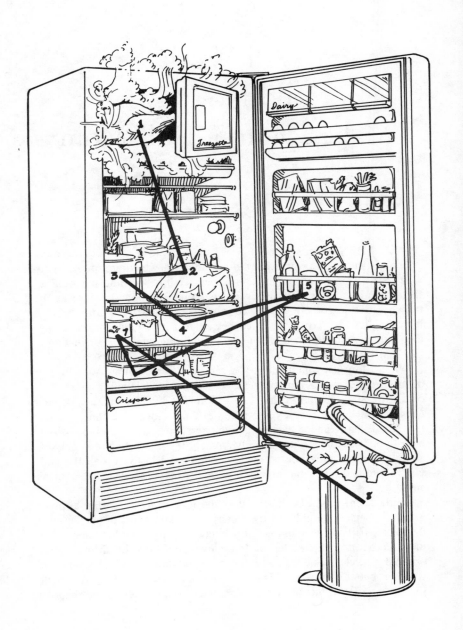

All Work
and No Play
Makes Mom a Dull Mom

WHEN Mom's work is done, she likes to relax by doing more work. She works hard at her hobbies, which are often strenuous, time-consuming, and repetitive, like weeding and pruning. In the garden, Mom has discovered perpetual motion, because as the tasks for one season are completed, a new season arrives, bringing with it new demands. To quote Chauncey Gardiner, "First comes spring, then summer, then fall, then winter, then spring again." Or something like that.

When Mom isn't gardening, she can be found canning, pickling, or otherwise preserving the fruits of her labors, and labeling them with cute little stick-on labels that say "From the kitchen of *Your Mom's Name Here*." Once you've left home, Mom loves sending you her homemade jams and jellies as a reminder that she's thinking of you, not of your waistline. Conveniently enough, these jars double as glasses, although by the time you've made enough toast to use up all the jam, you're probably too fat to want to invite anyone over for a drink anyway.

While Mom might be horrified at the idea of you sniffing airplane glue, she herself has inhaled the fumes of countless tins of shellac over the years, perhaps accounting for her tendency to leave her car keys in the icebox, and the butter in the glove compartment. Mom is the original recycler. She can see the potential lamp base in every old wooden butter churn. To her, a glass jar exists to be filled with seashells, colorful bits of glass, or imported soaps, often in the shape of seashells. But Mom's favorite way of turning ordinary household objects into exciting gift ideas is through decoupage. When you see big holes cut out of your favorite magazines, you know Mom has been there ahead of you with the good scissors. Everything is grist for Mom's decoupage mill, up to and including Michael Jackson. Before you can say, "Mom, where's my old Waltons lunch box?" it's an attractive handbag ready to be donated to the ladies' auxiliary hospital fund-raising raffle.

What with gardening, canning, refinishing furniture, and decoupaging, where does Mom find the time to knit all those sweaters? Well, the beauty of knitting is that you can do it while you're doing something else, like watching the news, waiting for a doctor's appointment, or having sex. (Just kidding, Mom. Honest.) Although Mom's earth-toned sweater may not go with your new neon socks, it's always nice to have something in your closet that was made with love. And when Mom's not there, it's comforting to feel her sweater hugging you with its long woolly arms.

All work and no play makes Mom a dull Mom. That's why she likes to get out on the links every now and then. Golf is one of Mom's favorite sports because it's a way to take a walk and do something else at the same time. Besides the exercise, she gets to talk to her friends without the constant interruption of kids, workmen, and pets. For more competitive Moms, tennis is a good substitute, and for more sedentary Moms, there's always bridge.

When Mom wants to escape from the leisure triangle of golf, tennis, and bridge, she turns to America's favorite recreational drug: alcohol. Once in a month of Sundays, Mom will have three, maybe four, drinks, and get down, get funky, and start doing old cheerleading routines from high school. But, of course, she's not drunk; she's just happy. The next morning, she acts like nothing happened, and flatly refuses to iron your gym uniform.

If Mom is good, she gets to go on a vacation with Dad, where she can play golf, tennis, and bridge. Whatever else she does, she's not telling, but from the number of tiny paper parasols in her luggage and the silly smile on her face when she and Dad talk about those romantic tropical nights, you can draw your own conclusions.

Working Mom

Easy-care hairstyle. Mom had it before Geraldine Ferraro.

Dress-for-success suit.

Mom washed the breakfast dishes before she left for the office.

Briefcase for stuff that won't fit in purse.

Oversize purse. See pages 46 and 47.

Baby doesn't want Mom to go bye-bye; uses Mom's skirt to deliver message.

Low-heeled shoes with plenty of arch support.

She Works Hard
for the Money

MOM works hard at whatever she does, whether it's getting every last crumb out of the toaster oven, driving the big rigs, or invading the Falklands. Just ask Maggie Thatcher.

Some Moms rule countries, like Golda Meir, Indira Gandhi, and Lady Macbeth. Some make discoveries, like Madame Curie, Margaret Mead, and Helena Rubinstein. Some make music, like Chrissie Hynde, Grace Slick, Yoko Ono, and Big Mama Thornton.

But if yours is the average working Mom, she's usually physically unavailable for at least eight hours out of every weekday. During this time, you tend to lose a lot more things than you would normally, and have this terrible feeling that there's nothing to eat in the house, except a lot of groceries.

No matter what her job, Mom must be prepared to receive phone calls from every member of her family regarding the whereabouts of lost items and vital phone numbers such as that of the pizza take-out place, which fell behind the icebox when you were ransacking the cupboard. This places an extra burden on Moms who are lawyers, movie stars, or astronauts, to name just a few.

Nevertheless, it's good for us all to have a working Mom, because not only does it boost the economy, it also teaches you to shift for yourself, and take a little responsibility around here.

When the shoe's on the other foot and you're working, Mom knows better than to bother you with inconsequential phone calls, and only interrupts you when it's something really important, like do you still want her to save that cute little green taffeta dress that you wore to the freshman prom because she's cleaning out your closet and needs to know what to do with it right now.

Mom is very proud of your work, even though she's not quite sure what it is. And whenever you're having difficulties with your boss, she's always standing by, ready to call him up and give him a piece of her mind. But if you're happy, she's happy. All she wants is for you to be the best at whatever you do—no pressure there, especially if you're a lawyer, a movie star, or an astronaut.

A Mom's Work Is Never Done

WHILE we agree that a woman's place is in the House and Senate, even working Moms must spend a portion of their waking hours dealing with the business of running a household. Housework consists of a series of repetitive tasks. No matter how neatly Mom makes beds, there are those who insist on sleeping in them and messing them up, so that they have to be made all over again in the morning. Many Moms, however, have developed the uncanny ability to sleep in a bed without mussing the sheets. This comes in especially handy when Mom has had a fight with Dad and wants to go sleep in the guest room without her children finding out.

This self-effacing style of housekeeping could best be described as the Deerslayer school of housework, in which Mom creeps stealthily through the house, following her own well-worn trails, disturbing things as little as possible, much as the Red Indian moved silently through the forest without breaking a twig. Mom is never the first person to toss a dirty Kleenex into a freshly emptied wastebasket, even if it means carrying her children's used tissues from room to room.

Borrowing a leaf from another classic, Mom is fond of emulating Tom Sawyer, who whitewashed the idea of work, making it seem like fun. A quick-witted Mom can have her children clamoring to be allowed to perform simple tasks such as ironing napkins. This enthusiasm, however, is short-lived, and Mom must soon resort to threats of cutting off your Twinkies in order to get you to set the table. "What do you think I'm running here—a hotel?"

Another one of Mom's literary influences is *Das Kapital*. There is no Marxist like a Mom. She fervently believes in the Marxist tenet "from each according to his ability, to each according to his needs." When asked why you have to do the dishes while your baby brother gets to throw his Slinky down the stairs, Mom's answer is, "Because you're bigger," or, on days when Mom is feeling especially witty, "Shut up and keep swimming."

On particularly trying days, Mom's responses take on a Zen-like quality. If you want to be introduced to Mom the Zen Master, just ask her the same question a thousand times, and she'll eventually reply, "Because I said so."

Although it is a rare soul who greets defrosting the refrigerator or cleaning the oven with a song in their heart and a smile on their lips, the fact remains that no one, except possibly Phyllis Diller, likes to live in a dirty house. That's why we'll pay people good money to come to our house and do what Mom used to do for love.

Close-up on the Dust Bunny

CONSIDER the dust bunny. It toils not, neither does it spin. In fact, not unlike a teen-ager, the dust bunny (*lepus dustus*) leads a lazy, sluggish, and totally unproductive life, hiding away in corners, where it never gets any exercise and probably ruins its only pair of eyes reading in poor light. It is closely related to the dust mouse and dust kitty, whose native habitat includes all of the continental United States, and Alaska and Hawaii. Their Canadian cousin is known as the dust beaver; their British brother is the dust hare; while Down Under, where everything is bigger, they are affectionately termed the dust wallaby; and we don't know what they're called in Japan. But whether they've set up housekeeping under a couch or behind the chifforobe, Mom considers it open season on these pesky little critters. She will often break off in the middle of a conversation to stare distractedly across the room and then leap out of her seat and begin poking under the sofa with a rolled-up magazine, or any other makeshift implement handy. Mom's efforts to decimate the dust bunny population are futile, however, as they breed as rapidly as their namesakes. Scientists say that after a nuclear holocaust, only the cockroach will survive. Mom knows better. She's betting on the dust bunny.

How to Shop
like a Mother

TWO thirds of Mom's life is spent shopping. This is because groceries, no matter how long their individual shelf life may be, seem only to remain on Mom's shelves for an hour or two before they disappear entirely, and need to be replaced, thus beginning the shopping cycle anew.

Mom's favorite fantasy is to make one big shopping trip in which she would buy enough staples to last a lifetime, but even in her fantasy, she comes home to discover that she's out of paper towels.

A word to the wise: Mom would do well to take into account the Lea & Perrins principle, according to which seldom-used items such as Worcestershire sauce, Tabasco, and arrowroot disappear immediately before a shopping trip, only to reappear as soon as Mom comes home with their replacements.

However, Mom can get a lot of satisfaction out of specials and bargains. Mom will always drive an extra ten miles out of her way to attend a shrimp riot, especially if they're giving extra green stamps.

A lot of Mom's shopping involves you. Despite your protests, she insists that it's impossible to buy you shoes without having your foot there in the store. Throughout your childhood, Mom buys you things you want, things you need, and things you don't want (like things you need).

Mom favors wardrobe basics that are practical and durable, and that go with everything. You just want what everybody else is wearing, and if they all jumped off a cliff wearing leg warmers in the summertime, you would too.

Lucky Dad doesn't have to take his foot to the store. Mom buys practically everything for him, except his suits and golf clubs. In some families, Mom buys all the gifts for everyone to give to everyone else, which can lead to a great deal of confusion when people can't remember which people they're supposed to thank for which gift. In the end, they usually wind up thanking Mom, who, in typical Mom fashion, replies, "Oh, don't thank me. Thank whomever the gift's from."

Leisure Mom

Mom's good coat reaches just to her knees, so she opted for her car coat, which she'll leave in the car.

Mom used hot rollers, just for tonight.

Plastic bangles from K mart perk up Mom's outfit and are safe for Baby.

Baby leaves a forget-me-not, but it's no big deal, because Mom's evening skirt is a polyester blend that only looks like taffeta.

Holds Mom's glasses and driver's license in case Dad has one too many.

Clip-on buckles transform daytime shoes.

Crybaby Mom

WHEN Junior cries, Mom is always there to offer comfort. But what about when Mom cries? And cries, and cries? In other words, suppose you have the kind of Mom who cries easily, for instance, when Walter Cronkite retired? What do you do?

Some children find themselves at their wit's end in this kind of situation, unable to quell Mom's tears with either a nice warm mug of Earl Grey tea, or a quickly improvised headstand.

Here are a few suggestions, guaranteed to stanch the floodwaters of even the Niagara Falls genus of Crybaby Mom.

First, check Mom all over to make sure the problem is not physical. Suggest that she loosen her clothing. The problem may be shoes that are pinching or a girdle that's riding up. Then again, it could just be the heartbreak of cellulite that's making her sob. Or maybe she simply can't stand the idea of running out of Bounce. In that case, you can probably chase those storm clouds away and bring out the sunshine with a little attention.

Offer Mom some Kleenex. Remember that Mom is in a fragile state, so make sure you're offering real tissues, not a paper towel, or something even more abrasive, like a pair of dirty jeans from the laundry room. Give Mom a hug. Be aware, however, that sympathy may make her cry harder, and you could be in for prolonged dampness.

Next, try crying along with Mom. Your tears may move her even more than your brother's touchdown, and she could end up ignoring her overflowing tear ducts in favor of your own.

If that doesn't work, try bribing her with the promise of breakfast in bed. Offer to do all the supper dishes for a week. But make sure you mean it, otherwise you might trigger a renewed outburst when she finds out you were only kidding.

If all else fails, resort to humor. Make funny faces. Jump up and down while making the faces. Tell a knock-knock joke, or do your impression of Dad. But again, be careful. This attempt to tickle Mom's funny bone can sometimes backfire and make Mom cry harder. Or it can also send Mom off into another mystifying mode of behavior where she may not be able to stop laughing. Should this happen, throw your hands up in desperation and announce that you are going to tell Dad.

But if none of these tactics work, don't worry. A good cry never hurt anyone. Mom will feel a lot better afterward, and may even want a nap. Just remember not to mention the name ''Walter Cronkite'' ever again.

Girl, You Are
a Woman Now

ONE day, strange things begin happening around your house. Those uncomfortable bumps on your chest are bringing about all sorts of illogical new rules. You can't sleep over at Jimmy's house anymore. No more roughhousing with your brothers. You are no longer a welcome guest on Daddy's lap. Mom buys you a trainer bra and keeps saying that you and she are going to have a little talk. You wonder what you did wrong this time. Then there's that day in biology class when they split up the boys and the girls and talk about your fallopian tubes. When the big day arrives, Mom finally has that talk with you, and refers to your condition as "the curse." She outfits you with a strange new accessory, and assures you that no one will be able to tell you're wearing it. You hope she's right, although it's hard to believe that a strip of cotton with some glue on it can make you feel as cool, calm, and confident as those gymnasts on TV. This is a big day for Mom, too, and she may even shed a tear. You're all grown up now, and once the tears subside, Mom will begin watching you like a hawk. So don't think you can pull any fast ones, because Mom wasn't born yesterday.

Momproofing
Your Room

WHEN Mom visits your room for an inspection, she's generally looking for two things: dust bunnies (kitties or mice; see Close-up on the Dust Bunny), and/or evidence of a secret social life, both of which can be swept under the rug.

To keep Mom happy and safe during those periodic visits to your inner sanctum, take note of the following valuable tips:

To disguise a dirty room, take broom and sweep junk on floor under bed. Stuff all clothes that have not been returned to proper places into laundry bag. Then, make sure bed is made, with hospital corners. Mom will be so distracted by this unusual display of motor skills that she will fail to notice offenses such as potato chip crumbs inside sheets.

Place Social Studies report entitled "The Importance of a Free Press" prominently on top of desk, so as to completely obscure evidence of obsessive phone calling, such as doodling.

To thwart Mom's career as a secret agent, padlock treasure chest containing steamy love letters referring to your "bedroom eyes." If unable to acquire a lock, keep written requests somewhere else to share passion, for instance inside your favorite doll—a hiding place you can utilize by twisting her head off, depositing secret items, and then putting her head back on. Some girls have even been known to enlist the aid of Teddy in their secret lives, cutting open a seam, stuffing personal treasures inside the little bear, and then sewing it up—which explains why Teddy has been known to accompany these girls into their adult lives.

If you're the kind of girl who stands in front of the mirror and practices smoking, then you'll need a safe place to hide those Kools. One tried-and-true area for the safekeeping of cigarettes is a hollowed-out copy of *Little Women*. Don't forget that smoking may be hazardous to your health, but Mom knew that before the Surgeon General.

Speaking of books, it's advisable to keep those of the X-rated variety well out of view, out on the windowsill, for example. Remember that unexpected foul weather may render page 56 of *Of Lust I Hunger* a thing of the past, but you knew that second paragraph backward and forward, anyway, didn't you?

Check to make sure Mom's panty hose have been returned before she finds them in someone else's dresser drawers, as if they just got up and walked there by themselves.

Cover electrical outlets so that Mom is unable to cause household brownouts by overloading circuits with auxiliary cleaning appliances, such as floor polishers or electric brooms.

Display a photo of Mom and Dad and all four grandparents on top of the dresser. If no such photo exists, substitute a photo of another family, such as the Waltons. Then it's okay to display a photo of The Cars as well.

Don't tempt Mom with a skateboard. Put it away, preferably out of reach, so as to avoid a potentially life-threatening accident when Mom decides to join the Pepsi generation.

Keep a fake diary in a top desk drawer. Keep the real one somewhere else.

A few final tips for the Mom-wary: Always be prepared for a surprise inspection. Keep a can of air freshener handy for emergency use. And, if the time ever comes when Mom does find something she shouldn't have—well, you've made your bed, young lady . . .

Mom's Purse

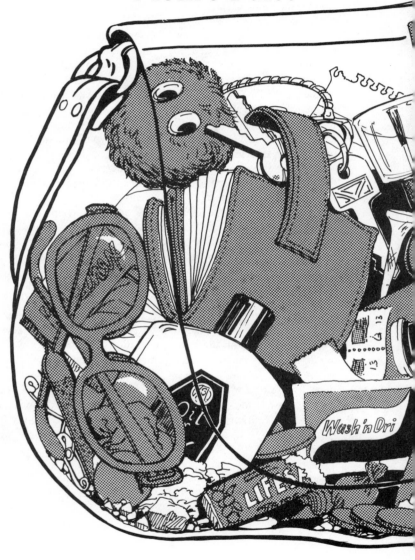

Pack Rat Mom

I T'S Mom's natural tendency to hold on to things, like your hand when you're crossing the street, the ceramic ashtray that you brought back from day camp, or the clipping from the time you were in the local paper for getting a speeding ticket. This hoarding instinct operates without any apparent regard to the size of the nest in which Mom finds herself, and continues, in fact flourishes, after the last fledgling has flown the coop.

Mom's inability to toss things out includes objects of sentimental value, such as a lock of hair from your first haircut, as well as objects of absolutely no value whatsoever, such as old keys that no one remembers what they open, but if you throw them out, you'll find out soon enough, young lady.

What kind of a hoarder is your Mom? Is there still room in the garage for Dad to park the car? Can you just start an impromptu game of Ping-Pong, or do you have to allow yourself a good two hours to clear off the table? Check the following categories for items that your Mom has saved. Give yourself one point for items saved in the first group, two for items saved in the second, three for items saved in the third, four for items saved in the fourth, and five for the last.

Add up the score and see where your Mom fits in on the hoarding scale:

Mouse	– 0 to 70
Chipmunk	– 71 to 100
Squirrel	– 101 to 135
Woodchuck	– 136 to 165
Pack Rat	– 166 or more

Things Mom Saves

Necessities of Daily Life (one point each)
    String
    Rubber bands
    Buttons
    Rags
    Old rags
    Grease
    Old coffee cans, to save grease in
    Jars
    Lids for other jars
    Aluminum foil (which many Moms persist in calling tinfoil)
    Plastic bags
    Paper bags
    Garbage bags
    Garbage bag ties
    Garbage ("Don't throw out those eggshells, they're perfect for my compost heap.")

Every Now and Then (two points each)
    Wrapping paper and ribbons
    Magazines
    Newspapers
    Informative newspaper clippings
    Green or any kind of stamps
    Chinese take-out soy sauce and mustard
    Wash 'n Dri towelettes from BBQ take-out places
    Straws
    Used plastic glasses and cutlery, which Mom collects after the party, washes, and saves

Sentimental Value (four points each)
    Report cards
    Old greeting and Christmas cards (sometimes saved for sentimental reasons, these can also be recycled for decoration)
    Baby teeth
    Pressed flowers
    Figurines from Mom's wedding cake

Once in a Blue Moon (three points each)

    Empty Aunt Jemima bottles

    Empty Honey Bear bears

    Egg cartons

    Little baskets fruit comes in

    Any basket anything comes in

    Clothes that Mom can't fit into but will after she goes on that diet

    Clothes she doesn't want Dad to wear but is afraid he'll realize they're missing someday and complain about it

    Clothes she's planning to give to Goodwill when she has enough

Absolutely No Value (five points each)

    Dead batteries just in case you run out, in which case you might try them again

    Pieces of hardware that you don't know what they are and you don't know what they fit

    Electrical gadgets that you don't know what they are and you don't know what they fit

    Broken ceramics that you've been meaning to glue back together but you don't have all the pieces anyway

    One shoe in case you find the other one

    An excess number of eyeglass cases

    Bottles of ink, even though no one in the house has a fountain pen

Fifty Ways to Leave
Your Mother

L IFE'S funny. Remember the day Mom first took you to play group and left you there? Remember that awful empty feeling in the pit of your stomach? You couldn't understand why Mom didn't want you around the house anymore, helping her in all sorts of useful ways, like coloring in the blank spots on the wallpaper with your new box of Crayolas.

You're afraid that maybe you'll never see Mom again and have to spend the rest of your formative years in the sandbox, hiding from that little kid with the big dump truck who kicked sand in your face when that scary lady that Mom left you with wasn't looking.

But only a week later, you cried when Mom came to pick you up early, because Miss Schreiber promised you could be the next one to play with the dump truck if you stopped kicking sand in Robbie's face.

No matter how independent and adventurous you are, your first sleep-over away from Mom can be a harrowing experience, sending many home in tears, clutching their blankies. Then, before you know it, you're calling up and begging to be allowed to stay another night, even if it's a school night. ("Honest, Mom, Sally and I are studying for the French quiz together. We're just watching *Lace II* because they speak French in it.")

Small wonder that they made a horror movie called *Sleepaway Camp*. It's an awfully long time to be separated from your room, your radio, your refrigerator, and your Mom. Plus, you have to undress in front of strangers, call yourself a Chipmunk, and eat mystery meat. But by the end of the summer, you find yourself crying real tears when you have to say "Chip chip, yip yip, see ya next summer" to your fellow Chipmunks and go home to Mom.

Every time you leave Mom, it gets easier, until you find yourself thinking about nothing but leaving Mom. Whether it's college, the army, marriage, or getting your own apartment, there must be fifty ways to leave your mother. You just . . .

Go to school, fool
Get your own flat, Matt
Shake hands with Uncle Sam, Pam
And go away to sea.

Run away, May
Run amok, Buck
Get hitched, Mitch
Just listen to me.

Thumb a ride, Clyde
Hop a freight, Nate
Get a Eurailpass, lass
And visit Italy.

Pitch a tent, Kent
Paddle your own canoe, Sue
Take a slow boat to China, Dinah
Be sure to stay for tea.

Become a nun, hon
Become a monk, punk
Go to jail, Gail
And throw away the key.

Have a kid, Sid
Cohabitate, Kate
Get an MBA, Ray
And be a VP at GE.

Make some dough, Moe
Buy a van, Stan
Become a Moonie, Junie
Set yourself free.

Moms
Will Be Moms

ONCE a Mom, always a Mom. You can grow up and move away from home and become the president of a multinational corporation, with your picture on the cover of *Savvy* magazine. But chances are, whenever Mom comes to visit, she'll still be mothering you. She doesn't know how you'd get along without her, perhaps because she's never seen you do it.

When you have Mom as a houseguest, you immediately regress to childhood, becoming your old forgetful, irresponsible, messy, and self-ish self. And Mom becomes a self you've never seen before. She has a distressing tendency to ignore all the rules she told you to follow the first time you slept over at your girl friend's house.

She criticizes your cooking, housekeeping, and laundry methods, borrows your clothes, and plays your stereo, which she calls a hi-fi, without asking you first how to operate it.

In fact, even normally mechanically minded Moms seem to have enormous difficulty with any electronic equipment or household appliances that have not been approved by the Bureau of Mom Research. She complains that "they don't work right," and compares them unfavorably with her own back home. If you point out that her dishwasher is as old as you are, she's bound to observe that "they just don't make 'em like they used to."

And, oddly enough, the very same Mom who told you that curiosity killed the cat can't control her own when introduced to your friends, particularly if you happen to be unmarried and the friends are male. Count yourself lucky if she refrains from recording their blood types and checking to see if there's any history of hemophilia or Tay-Sachs disease in their families.

Even with other friends, Mom often asks embarrassing questions, like "Are you two married, or just roommates?" And when you introduce her to a gay friend, she spends the evening matchmaking between you and him.

If you're living with someone, Mom just can't keep herself from wondering aloud if you wouldn't be happier if you were married. Once you are married, Mom frequently points out exactly how many child-bearing years, months, and days you have left before your biological clock runs down. When you do have children, her scorekeeping shifts to how many years she has left to spend with her grandchildren.

Your kids just adore Grandma, and wish you could be more like her. Grandma just can't deny her little sunshine anything, especially when she's requested to recount some horror story from your childhood, like the time you bit Bobby Cooney in the butt at your sixth birthday party and had to be spanked and sent upstairs to your room while everyone else had ice cream and cake. You'd worry that your Mom is spoiling your kids if it weren't for the fact that she reminds you so much of your own Grandma.

If Mom gets on your nerves occasionally, try not to overreact. She can't help being a Mom. It's hard for her to recognize that you're not still the cute little pink-and-white bundle who drooled on her shoulder on the way home from the hospital, because, deep in her heart, that's the picture of you she'll always carry with her.

It's not true that old Moms can't learn new tricks. But it's a slow process. Most Moms respond better to rewards than scolding. And slapping Mom's hand while saying "no, no" is seldom effective. Remember, repetition brings results. If you want Mom to relate to you as the grown-up you hope you are, just repeat calmly but firmly what it is you want her to do, and sooner or later she'll think she thought of it.

When introducing Mom to new things, do it gradually. Pressing *Fear and Loathing in Las Vegas* into Mom's hands and telling her that it explains your life-style in a nutshell is not recommended. Give her a copy of *My Mother, My Self* instead.

Do your best to convince your Mom to stop using outmoded expressions like "colored people," "fairy," "icebox," "groovy," and "bummer." But don't attempt to change her too much. Mom should act her age, not her shoe size. A slamdancing Mom is not a pretty sight.

Try as you will, there's one thing you can never take away from Mom, and that's her right to ask you to show her your tongue at any time. So be ready to open wide and say "Aah," because Mother knows best.

Dial "M"
for Mother

SHE wasn't called "Ma Bell" for nothing. According to Alexander Graham Bell's mother, her son invented the phone for one reason: so he could call her. When you're away from home, the phone is another umbilical cord stretching between you and Mom.

Remember the first telephone you ever had? It was soft baby-blue plastic, and nobody ever phoned you on it. Instead, they phoned Mom on her phone and took her attention away from you while you were trying to show her your drawing of a fire truck. In self-defense, you learned to say "Hi, Grandma, I miss you" no matter who was on the other end of the phone.

You can get away with this for a couple of years, and by then, if you're lucky, some of the calls will no doubt be for you. Mom is excited, because her little answering service is growing up. She will now be able to trust you to take messages until you hit puberty, at which point an all-out War of the Wires breaks out between you and Mom.

Commencement of hostilities is usually sparked by Mom's inability to understand why you have to spend all night talking on the phone to someone you see all day in school. You counterattack by grunting at your mother's friends when they call, but Mom outflanks you by revoking your telephone privileges for a week.

And then, things get worse. Mom gets chummy with your phonemates and starts quizzing them about your social life. Worse yet, when that certain somebody phones. Mom can't resist announcing to the world at large, ''I think this is the call you've been waiting for.'' And whenever you're on the phone, you live in constant fear that Mom may pick up the extension.

This sorry state of affairs continues until you move out and get a phone of your own, at which point Mom's slogan becomes ''Reach out and wake somebody up.''

A Blast from the Past: Smells That Remind You of Mom

IF a picture is worth a thousand words, a smell is worth a thousand pictures. If you don't believe this, just sniff a piece of chalk. Better yet, sample some of the Mom-reminiscent scratch-and-sniff patches on this page. Each is redolent of a different aspect of having a Mom. Put them all together, and they smell M-O-T-H-E-R.

Scratch 'N' Sniff

Classic Mom

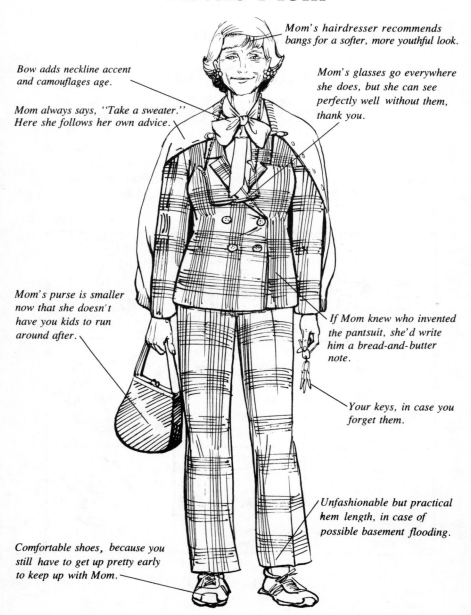

Mom's hairdresser recommends bangs for a softer, more youthful look.

Bow adds neckline accent and camouflages age.

Mom's glasses go everywhere she does, but she can see perfectly well without them, thank you.

Mom always says, "Take a sweater." Here she follows her own advice.

Mom's purse is smaller now that she doesn't have you kids to run around after.

If Mom knew who invented the pantsuit, she'd write him a bread-and-butter note.

Your keys, in case you forget them.

Unfashionable but practical hem length, in case of possible basement flooding.

Comfortable shoes, because you still have to get up pretty early to keep up with Mom.

Remembering
Mama

YOUR Mom is the one person in your life you're least likely to forget. However, you'd be surprised how easy it is for you to forget those special occasions that mean so much to Mom—especially when she's not around to remind you by dropping subtle hints such as baking herself a birthday cake and asking you to decorate it so it'll be a surprise.

Of course, your mother will always forgive you for forgetting one of "her" days. But after all she's done for you, surely you can take time out from your busy schedule to pick up the phone and give her a call. And if not, you'll have to live with the guilt for the rest of the year.

In fact, Mother's Day was invented by somebody who forgot their Mom's birthday and was looking for a way to make it up to her. In pagan times, Mother's Day often lasted a whole week, but then so did childbirth. In ancient Rome, the festivities honoring motherhood were known as the Hilaria, because even way back before Christ, Mom didn't like a grouchy face.

During the Middle Ages (coincidentally, a time in Mom's life when she needs to be remembered most), Christians set aside a special day to venerate the Mother of God. In England, the fourth Sunday in Lent became known as Mothering Sunday, because it was the custom for children who had left home to return on that day to visit their mothers, bringing with them a rich fruitcake. Typically, tradition prevented Mom from eating the cake until Lent was over, but as Mom always says, it's the thought that counts.

The American version of Mother's Day was started in 1868 by Anna Reeves Jarvis of Grafton, West Virginia, who hoped that the holiday would bring together families divided by the Civil War. "Just because there's been a little war doesn't mean we can't all get along," she said.

But it was her daughter, Anna Jr., who really went to bat for Mother's Day and made it stick. She was aided in her efforts by Mary Towles Sasseen, a teacher in Henderson, Kentucky, and by Fred E. Hering of South Bend, Indiana. Interestingly enough, none of them were mothers; which, when you think about it, makes a lot of sense, because what Mom would have time for that sort of thing?

By 1911, Mother's Day was being celebrated in all states of the Union, and in 1914, President Woodrow Wilson, another nonmother, issued a proclamation setting aside the second Sunday in May "as a public expression of our love and reverence for the mothers of our country." His mother said, "Woody, you shouldn't have," but she was secretly pleased.

In 1934, the U.S. Post Office further commemorated the holiday by issuing a three-cent stamp depicting the famed portrait of his mother by James McNeill Whistler. Mrs. Whistler was not available for comment; but we all know what she would have said.

Unwritten law decrees that all Moms must say "You shouldn't have" when presented with a gift; otherwise they are not allowed in the Mom Union. Under the same regulations, Moms must say, "All I want is your love and respect," when asked what they would like for Mother's Day.

Do not be taken in. This is just a formality. Mom would really like a dozen red roses or, failing that, something you made yourself—preferably something she can carry in her purse and show to the other Moms, like a rock with her name on it. Or perhaps a dozen roses *and* a rock. A handy rule of thumb for Mother's Day gift-giving: At Christmastime, good children get more presents; on Mother's Day, bad children should give more presents.

TV Moms

W HEN TV first arrived in households all over America, Mom was thrilled to find she now had a built-in baby-sitter. She could park the kids in front of the set and forget about 'em. The TV set itself became a surrogate Mom—and then there were those little black-and-white Moms on TV who always knew how to handle any family crisis without mussing their hair or getting a crease in their spotless shirtwaist dresses.

It took quite a few years before Mom realized that this was tough competition. Even though Father knew best, Margaret Anderson always knew better. It was hard for real moms to live up to the perfect Mom as shown on TV. When her kids wondered why she wasn't more like Donna Reed, she didn't know how to tell them that, unlike Donna, she didn't have her own costume designer, makeup man, hairstylist, dresser, set decorator, lighting designer, and scriptwriter to make her look great.

And when she wanted her kids to act like Donna's TV kids, Paul Petersen and Shelley Fabares, it didn't occur to her that they might have been better behaved if they were paid a substantial salary plus residuals for doing what they were told.

This breakdown in communication was the beginning of the generation gap, which ultimately led to long hair, campus riots, the burning of the Bank of America, and Earth Shoes. Poor Donna Reed. If she had only known what effect she and the others of her ilk would have, like a good mother, she would have been the first to point out that nobody's perfect.

While ''Father Knows Best'' made no mention of what Mom knew in the title, other shows didn't even have a Mom in the cast. Apparently,

America found both credible and entertaining the spectacle of good ol' Dad raising the kids by himself, often with help from an amusing oldster such as Uncle Charley on "My Three Sons" or an amusing ethnic such as Peter the Chinese houseboy on "Bachelor Father," where Dad wasn't even a real Dad, just an uncle with an overdeveloped sense of responsibility.

As television became more and more a part of our everyday lives, it seemed to get farther and farther away from everyday reality. Some TV Moms were gifted with supernatural powers, like Samantha and her own mother, Endora, on "Bewitched." Still, Samantha was a conformist at heart, and most of her witchcraft went into living as normal a suburban life as possible, much to her mother's dismay. And even though Morticia Addams of "The Addams Family" may have been weird, there's no doubt that she loved little Wednesday and Pugsley just as much as your Mom loved you, and would certainly feed Pugsley's pet octopus if he forgot.

Either a new high or a new low, depending on your point of view, was reached in the portrayal of Mom on television with the creation of the short-lived comedy series, "My Mother the Car," in which the hero's mother was reincarnated as an old jalopy. This show was later sold to Indian television as "My Mother the Cow."

It wasn't until the early seventies that a believable Mom, with human virtues and foibles, showed up on the small screen. First to appear was Rhoda's mother, Ida Morgenstern, on "The Mary Tyler Moore Show," the first Jewish mother on TV since Molly Goldberg. She was followed by Edith Bunker, a dithery dingbat with a charm all her own, whose slavish devotion to her husband, Archie, sharply pointed up the flaws in the traditionally subservient female role. And then there's Maude, enterprising, socializing, everything but compromising—right on, Maude!

The eighties offer the TV viewer a wealth of rerun Moms, plus enough true-to-life single-parent Moms, like "Kate and Allie," to keep pace with current statistics. On "Cheers," the character played by Rhea Perlman has broken new ground by becoming a Mom without the benefit of a husband.

Recently, family shows seem to have given way to action-adventure series where all the main characters are detectives, even the car. Some of the detectives, like Mary Beth Lacey, are Moms. Some of them have Moms, like Amanda King's mother, Dotty West.

As we write, yet another twist on a tired theme is being tested: an

THE MOM BOOK   63

action-adventure series featuring a mother-daughter detective team—''Me
and Mom.'' But whether this series survives or not, as long as people
all over the world still love Lucy, there'll always be at least one Mom
on the tube.

In studying TV Moms, we noticed that most of them are known as
either Mom or Mrs. (Dad's Last Name Here). Unless their name is
specifically mentioned in the title of the show, it's easy to forget. You
may remember Mama, but who remembers her name was Marta Hansen? Quick, for everything behind the curtain, what was Mary Tyler
Moore's mother's name? And ''Mrs. Richards'' doesn't count.

How many TV Moms do you remember? For each of the categories
below, name the show on which each Mom appeared. Answers begin
on page 66, but no fair peeking, because when you cheat, you only
cheat yourself.

Perfect Moms
1. Harriet Nelson
2. Margaret Anderson
3. June Cleaver
4. Donna Stone
5. Winifred Gillis
6. Peg Riley
7. Alice Mitchell
8. Dorothy Baxter
9. Margaret Williams
10. Kathy Williams
11. Marion Cunningham

Single Moms
1. Carolyn Muir
2. Constance Mackenzie Carson
3. Doris Martin
4. Julia Baker
5. Ann Romano
6. Alice Hyatt
7. Elaine Nardo
8. Carla Tortelli
9. Kate McArdle
10. Allie Lowell

Minority Moms
1. Molly Goldberg
2. Marta Hansen
3. Louise Jefferson
4. Florida Evans
5. Julia Baker
6. Ida Morgenstern
7. Clair Huxtable

Zany Moms
1. Gracie Allen
2. Blondie Bumstead
3. Lucy Ricardo
4. Samantha Stevens
5. Mary Hartman
6. Mork

Moms-in-Law
1. Lily Ruskin
2. Endora
3. Eve Hubbard
4. Kaye Buell
5. Mama Jefferson
6. Martha Shumway

Working Moms
1. Gracie Allen
2. Julia Baker
3. Doris Martin
4. Phyllis Lindstrom
5. Ann Romano
6. Alice Hyatt
7. Elaine Nardo
8. Elyse Keaton
9. Gloria Stivic
10. Carla Tortelli
11. Mary Beth Lacey
12. Kate McArdle
13. Gladys Crabtree

Sensible Moms
1. Kate Lawrence
2. Muriel Rush
3. Allie Lowell

Schizo Moms

Each of these actresses played more than one Mom during her TV career. Name the different shows on which each appeared.

1. Lucille Ball
2. Cloris Leachman
3. June Lockhart
4. Donna Reed
5. Nanette Fabray
6. Nancy Walker
7. Meredith Baxter Birney

Prairie Moms
1. Ruth Martin
2. Kate McCoy
3. Kate Bradley
4. Victoria Barkley
5. Olivia Walton
6. Grandma Walton
7. Caroline Ingalls

Power Moms
1. Miss Ellie
2. Alexis Carrington Colby Dexter
3. Angela Channing

Surrogate Moms
1. Rin Tin Tin
2. Peter Tong
3. "Bub" O'Casey
4. Uncle Charley
5. Aunt Bee
6. Hazel Burke
7. Granny Clampett
8. Katy Holstrum
9. Uncle Martin
10. Giles French
11. Mrs. Livingston
12. Phoebe Figalilly
13. Alice Nelson
14. Edna Garrett
15. Benson
16. Tony Micelli

Soap Opera Moms

There are a lot of Moms on soap operas, wed and unwed. However, if we watched soap operas enough to figure out whose Mom was who, and who was lying or had amnesia about whose Mom they were or weren't, we'd end up spending so much time watching soap operas that we'd never get this book done. If you know, please fill us in—that is, if you can tear yourself away from the set long enough to write.

Match Each TV Mom with Her Description

1. Edith Bunker
2. Laura Petrie
3. Shirley Partridge
4. Lily Munster
5. Morticia Addams
6. Mama (Ellen and Eunice's Mom)
7. Maude Findlay
8. Wilma Flintstone
9. Jane Jetson
10. Carol Brady
11. Amanda Spock

A. Prehistoric Mom
B. Weird Mom
C. Bossy Mom
D. Feminist Mom
E. Sexy Mom
F. Vampire Mom
G. Singing Mom
H. Futuristic Mom
I. Dingbat Mom
J. Star Trek Mom
K. Stepmom

(Correct answers on following page)

Answers

Perfect Moms
1. "Ozzie and Harriet"
2. "Father Knows Best"
3. "Leave It to Beaver"
4. "The Donna Reed Show"
5. "The Many Loves of Dobie Gillis"
6. "The Life of Riley"
7. "Dennis the Menace"
8. "Hazel"
9. "Make Room for Daddy" (first wife)
10. "Make Room for Daddy" (second wife)
11. "Happy Days"

Single Moms
1. "The Ghost and Mrs. Muir"
2. "Peyton Place"
3. "The Doris Day Show"
4. "Julia"
5. "One Day at a Time"
6. "Alice"
7. "Taxi"
8. "Cheers"
9. "Kate and Allie"
10. "Kate and Allie"

Minority Moms
1. "The Goldbergs"
2. "I Remember Mama"
3. "The Jeffersons"
4. "Good Times"
5. "Julia"
6. "Rhoda"
7. "The Cosby Show"

Zany Moms
1. "The George Burns and Gracie Allen Show"
2. "Blondie"
3. "I Love Lucy"
4. "Bewitched"
5. "Mary Hartman, Mary Hartman"
6. "Mork and Mindy"

Moms-in-Law
1. "December Bride"
2. "Bewitched"
3. "The Mothers-in-Law"
4. "The Mothers-in-Law'
5. "The Jeffersons"
6. "Mary Hartman, Mary Hartman"

Working Moms
1. "The George Burns and Gracie Allen Show"
2. "Julia"
3. "The Doris Day Show"
4. "Phyllis"
5. "One Day at a Time"
6. "Alice"
7. "Taxi"
8. "Family Ties"
9. "Gloria"
10. "Cheers"
11. "Cagney and Lacey"
12. "Kate and Allie"
13. "My Mother the Car"

Sensible Moms
1. "Family"
2. "Too Close for Comfort"
3. "Kate and Allie"

Schizo Moms
1. Mom Lucy Ricardo on "I Love Lucy"; Mom Lucy Carmichael on "The Lucy Show"; Lucille Carter on "Here's Lucy."
2. Timmy's Mom, Ruth Martin, on "Lassie"; Bess's Mom on "The Mary Tyler Moore Show" and "Phyllis."
3. Timmy's other Mom, Ruth Martin, on "Lassie"; Mom Maureen Robinson on "Lost in Space."
4. Mom Donna Stone on "The Donna Reed Show"; Miss Ellie on "Dallas."
5. Mom Nanette McGovern on "Yes, Yes Nanette"; Mary's Mom, Dotty Richards, on "The Mary Tyler Moore Show." Ann Romano's Mom, Katherine Romano, on "One Day at a Time."
6. Rhoda's mother on "The Mary Tyler Moore Show" and "Rhoda." Mom Nancy Kitteridge on "The Nancy Walker Show."
7. Mom Nancy Lawrence Maitland on "Family"; Mom Elyse Keaton on "Family Ties."

Prairie Moms
1. "Lassie"
2. "The Real McCoys"
3. "Petticoat Junction"
4. "The Big Valley"
5. "The Waltons"
6. "The Waltons"
7. "Little House on the Prairie"

Power Moms
1. "Dallas"
2. "Dynasty"
3. "Falcon Crest"

Surrogate Moms
1. "The Adventures of Rin Tin Tin"

2. "Bachelor Father"
3. "My Three Sons"
4. "My Three Sons"
5. "The Andy Griffith Show"
6. "Hazel"
7. "The Beverly Hillbillies"
8. "The Farmer's Daughter"
9. "My Favorite Martian"
10. "Family Affair"
11. "The Courtship of Eddie's Father"
12. "Nanny and the Professor"
13. "The Brady Bunch"
14. "The Facts of Life"
15. "Benson"
16. "Who's the Boss?"

Answers to Matching TV Mom with Her Description:
1I, 2E, 3G, 4F, 5B, 6C, 7D, 8A, 9H, 10K, 11J.

Future Mom

ACCORDING to recently released classified documents from the navy, scientists are secretly at work on the prototype for the perfect Mom. While the Russians have reportedly created the first robot Mom, a snafu in programming has resulted in a model that is unable to stop ironing—perhaps allowing ingenious Americans to surge ahead in this important, high-stakes area.

Humorously dubbed "Betsy Ross" by her creators, the American mechanical Mom is well into the advanced stages of production, and may be on the market on a limited basis as early as 2010. Most impressive in its list of features are the following:

*Betsy is programmed with her very own weekly menu planner, featuring two hundred well-balanced variations on the three meals a day, with thousands of combinations thereof, including an instant menu retrieval file listing "150 Ways to Trick Dad into Eating Bell Peppers." This feature permits Mom to save the budget-minded family at least $100 per year by economizing in two ways: Bell peppers cost next to nothing, and subscriptions to certain magazines become a thing of the past.

*Betsy is user-friendly and capable of hugging and cuddling you when you're feeling blue, wake up from a nightmare, or fall down and hurt yourself. She also puts a Band-Aid on skinned knees and says, "Let me kiss the boo-boo."

*Betsy's shoes double as walking Dustbusters, absorbing layers of dirt and grime as she moves through the house, thus saving about $30 per year on vacuum cleaner bags.

*An unusual piece of headgear, a rearview mirror, allows Betsy to keep a constant eye on Junior, and everyone else, whether she's basting a turkey or polishing up that chafing dish. Watch out.

*Betsy can run a mail-order business out of her own body! The ability to store vast amounts of information inside the intricate career center of Mom's command unit allows this automaton to operate a successful home-based business that many mail-order barons would envy.

*Optional software includes a program that allows Betsy to do your homework, including New Math and diagramming sentences. However, the program is activated only when you remember to say "Please" and "Thank you."

A Note from Our Mothers

We just wanted to say that we think our daughters have out-done themselves with this Mom book thing they've been working so hard on.

It's very funny in parts, their friend Mary did some lovely illustrations, and we could find only one spelling mistake as of our tenth reading. All in all, they really did a wonderful job, although we don't know where they get some of those crazy ideas, certainly not from us.

In any case, we're very proud of them. But then we always knew they had it in them. And maybe now they'll have more time to sit down and write a letter to their mothers.

Sincerely,
Jean Jacklin
Eleanor Stillman
Sheila Beatts